Budget Like A Pro

Manage Your Money, Pay Off Your Debts, And Walk
The Road Of Financial Independence

Personal Finance Made Easy

Zoe McKey

Communication Coach and Social Development
Trainer

zoemckey@gmail.com
www.zoemckey.com

Thank you for choosing my book! I would like to show my appreciation for the trust you gave me by giving **FREE GIFTS** for you!

For more information visit: www.zoemckey.com

The checklist talks about *5 key elements of building self-confidence* and contains extra actionable worksheets with practice exercises for deeper learning.

Learn how to:

- Solve 80% of you self-esteem issues with one simple change
- Keep your confidence permanent without falling back to self-doubt
- Not fall into the trap of promising words
- Overcome anxiety
- Be confident among other people

The cheat sheet teaches you three key daily routine techniques to become more productive, have less stress in your life, and be more well-balanced. It also has a step-by-step sample sheet that you can fill in with your daily routines.

Discover how to:

- Overcome procrastination following 8 simple steps
- Become more organized
- Design your yearly, monthly, weekly and daily tasks in the most productive way.
- 3 easy tricks to level up your mornings

Table of Contents

Chapter 1: Money Myths

Let's take a moment to talk about what money myths are. As you grow up, you are constantly fed different ideas about money and finances. Since finances aren't often taught in school, you are left mirroring what your family has told you. And unfortunately, our families often aren't the best examples of how we should build wealth. Unless you grew up in a wealthy household which made great financial choices, mirroring your family's financial path can lead to you having a negative view of how money works.

The secret to making your wealth is not the amount of money you have, but the mindset toward it. Let's put this into perspective …

If you were a billionaire who'd lost almost all of their money, but was left with two million dollars, what would you think? You would think you were poor! Two million seems like a huge amount of money, but compared to billions, it is nothing. If an actual billionaire lost all his money, he wouldn't think he was poor. He would think of strategies to recreate his wealth. This is what we call a millionaire mindset. Money is just a tool; the real power resides in the knowledge of how to create money.

Most people believe having a few thousand dollars is successful. If you want to be wealthy, you need to change your mindset about money.

We'll talk about money expectations a little later in the book, but for now, let's steer back to how money myths can hurt our wealth and lead us further into debt. Day in and day out, we tell ourselves lies to justify our bad financial decisions. Below, I will highlight some of the most common money myths we all find ourselves using.

"It was on sale."

One day, I went out shopping with my friends at the nearest mall. I wasn't really expecting to buy something, because at the time I was working a few jobs and just trying to stay afloat in terms of money. Knowing that if I bought another new top my roommates would hound me, I just went to enjoy the company of my friends.

We were walking through the mall when my friends started getting really excited. I looked in the direction they were staring and found the sign: "Big Sale, Up to 75% off!" I immediately went to the store with them and started looking through the racks. When I found a dress I had been eyeing in the window, I looked at the price tag.

It was originally $200, but was now on sale for $50! I could not pass up the deal and quickly purchased the dress.

Looking back on that incident, I realize how stupid it is that we all purchase so much stuff on sale. This is one of the greatest traps in our financial lives, and yet we all do it. Look around your household and in your closet. How many things did you purchase not because you needed them, but because they were on sale?

Sales are one of the leading causes of debt. We build debt based on things we don't actually need, but buy anyway because we think we are getting a good deal.

When we find ourselves perusing the sales rack, we think we have a saving mindset. We believe that we are saving money by buying items from the sale or clearance section. We get in a sale frenzy and start talking about all the money we are saving!

When I bought the dress for $50, I thought I saved $150, but I actually did not. You are not saving money by shopping in the clearance section of the store. Best-case scenario, you are just spending less money.

If a $200 dress is on sale for $50, you did not save $150. You spent $50! It is still spending, no matter if it was on sale or not. In other words, our saving mindset is actually a spending mindset when it comes to sales. Whenever we shop for things that are not necessary, our spending mindset is activated, even if we save 99% on the price.

However, if you do need to go to the store, be aware of the items surrounding you. When you see something you want or like, ask yourself, "Do I truly need this?" or, "How often would I use this?"

Even if it only costs a few dollars, these things add up! Five dollars here, ten dollars there can add up to hundreds of dollars over the year. Before you purchase anything, make sure it is something you need or will use a lot. If you are in debt and trying to get out, spending on anything but essentials will just dig your financial hole even deeper.

"It was an emergency."

I had a friend growing up who absolutely loved to shop. Her parents would give her money quite frequently, and she would spend every penny of it. One day, she broke up with her boyfriend of a year. She stormed her slim self into my bedroom with a few bags of clothes from the nearest Nordstrom.

Shocked, I asked her, "Where did these clothes come from? Why did you buy these?" With a look on her face that told me she was taken aback, she exclaimed, "Me and Derek just broke up. I had to buy new outfits since I'm going back on the dating scene. It was an emergency!"

How many times have you had a bad day at work and reached for some extra quarters to buy a candy bar? Your bad day at work was an emergency for chocolate! You need to fill that void, right? No, not right.

There are two types of expenses: regular expenses and emergency expenses. When you have a regular expense, you pay it monthly or yearly. These types of expenses can include your car insurance, your rent, your groceries, your cell phone bill, or anything else you regularly pay and is an anticipated expense.

If you bought a brand new computer and it crapped out on you a few months later, that would be an emergency. It was a totally unexpected event. If you got in a car accident and had medical bills, that would also be an emergency. Any necessary, but unexpected expense is an emergency.

But a break-up with a significant other is not enough of an emergency to go out and buy a new wardrobe. And your favorite band coming to play a concert only an hour away from you is not an emergency and does not require you to buy tickets. If your old computer that is ten years past its trade-in date finally gets laid to rest, that should be an eventuality that you plan for.

Some people believe that they can take money out of their emergency fund whenever they exclaim that something is an emergency. First of all, you better have an emergency fund. If you don't, create one now. I will talk later in the book about how to set it up.

Second of all, emergency funds serve the purpose of aiding you when something dire and unexpected comes up. They are there for actual emergencies. Do not sabotage your peace of mind by emptying your emergency fund because you had a bad day. You'll have many bad days coming if you have no savings.

Do not empty your emergency fund for something that really is not needed! You will end up more worried than you started. Plan to use your emergency fund only when it is absolutely necessary.

"If I had more money ..."

A woman named Sharon Tirabassi was on welfare and struggling to make it as a single mother. Luck suddenly struck her one day and she found herself cashing in a check for $10 million. She'd won the lottery. Over the years, she spent this money on a fancy house, a new car, designer clothes, expensive trips, and handouts to family and friends.

Less than ten years went by and she was back riding the bus, working, and living in a rented house she couldn't call hers. She and her six children benefited from this lottery money, but then spent it all.

This is maybe the most-heard money myth today. Everyone always says that if they had more money, they would be happy, they could afford their house, they could take their family on vacations, and they wouldn't have to work so hard.

Let me tell you this secret: If you cannot manage the money you currently have, you won't be able to effectively manage more money. More money is not the solution. If you make more, you will spend more if you have no discipline.

You have to know how to use your finances effectively so that you are not finding yourself in debt. If you cannot keep $1000 from blowing in the wind, what is going to make $10,000 stay? Sharon's story above is the perfect example of how more money won't fix a bad financial mindset.

Thankfully, you won't end up doing what Sharon did. How do I know this? Because you are willing to learn. You purchasing my book is proof of that. I will provide you with the best, easy-to-follow tips to help you keep your money. You can also turn to Google and look up what you don't know. Lack of knowledge is not a good excuse these days. All the information you wish to know is so accessible. You do not need to be the Wolf of Wall Street to keep yourself on good financial terms. If you manage your money well, you don't need to fear you'll run out of it.

"I deserve it."

A woman I know fell on some hard times. Her husband pulled money out of their retirement fund and blew the equity of their home on buying a bigger fishing boat. He said he deserved it. He went on a fishing trip one day and never came back. This woman had to turn her life around and start working when she used to be a stay-at-home mom. There is no doubt that she was a hard worker and got dealt the short end of the stick in life, but when she found herself suddenly making a lot less money than what she was used to, she found herself in debt. Even though she was working and making money, she didn't know how to manage it. She didn't know where her new spending boundaries lay, so she often overspent her budget on non-essential stuff like getting her hair done or eating out too often.

She would complain about being in debt because she said that she deserved to make more money. She deserved to not have to worry about finances after being so royally screwed. By the way, she didn't deserve to be left bankrupt and alone by her husband. Don't get me wrong; she did not deserve what her husband did to her. It was simple cowardice.

But when it comes to finances, it is often not about what we deserve, but rather what we can or should afford. Most often, these concepts are not proportional. We often deserve much more than we can afford. Before material deserving, however, you should consider positioning your mental peace. Do you deserve the anxiety and stress coming from mismanaged money?

Even if you are the hardest-working person and you deserve some indulgences here and there, do you really need to buy that fifth purse or twentieth video game? The financial choices we make because we feel like we deserve new items are what get us deeper into debt.

Everyone should treat himself or herself. Don't go through life not treating yourself. Life is too short. But what is the better treat in your situation? Is it your *Call of Duty* deluxe expansion pack, or is it finding yourself debt-free?

Getting yourself out of debt and accumulating healthy savings will help you gain peace of mind. The small amount of satisfaction you experience when you buy that new game is not going to last. In fact, you are most likely going to feel even worse after you walk away from the store with the bag in your hand.

You deserve to be debt-free. You deserve peace of mind. But unless you are related to Bill Gates, you can't buy endless video games and other expensive items. Before you buy something else, think about *whether or not it is essential and it is going to get your further into debt*. If it is not essential and just worsens your financial situation, skip purchasing it.

"I don't make enough money to save."

Let me tell you a little bit about my own personal story. I lived on $200 a month. You read that right. Two hundred dollars! That is close enough to nothing. But even as I lived on $200 a month, I still put aside some money to save.

How did I do this? I kept a very strict budget. I lived in a cheap student hostel so I would not have to spend extra cash on expensive apartments. I worked constantly, even during high school, taking supplementary classes in hopes to change my situation. I bought the bare minimum when shopping. I lived on cheap bread and salami with water. I didn't buy sodas or coffees; I only bought what was necessary.

Even though this is an extreme situation, I had to live through it to get to where I am today. And the most important point to be made here is that even with nothing, I still saved money. I put aside some income so that one day, my situation would be better.

If you don't make a lot of money, you still need to find somewhere to save. Do you have a budget? Create one. Later in the book, I will tell you how exactly. So many people are in disbelief over where their money goes. Try anything you can to save some money so you can put away extra cash into savings. Stop buying coffees from places like Starbucks and Dunkin' Donuts. You can get a pack of coffee at Safeway at as little as four or five bucks. This pack will last you up to two months. Is it a bad coffee? It is. I'm not going to lie. But one can't have champagne tastes on a beer budget. Unfortunately. I know this more than anyone. I'm sorry I can't say something more encouraging. I won't sell lies. Until you make more money and get out of debt, you need to cut your expenses. There is no easy way around it.

Hey, on the bright side, I assure you that with focus and dedication, you can turn that sinking financial ship around. I fixed my finances, got out of debt, and have accrued more savings than my entire family in less than four years. How did I do it? Making the changes explained in this book.

Some quick saving tips, if you think you don't know from where to cut anymore: Buy items in bulk to save money. My mom used to buy all our staple foods when she got her pension at the beginning of the month. Milk, oil, butter, bread, some cheap meat... all in bulk deals and into the cart, then into the freezer. They weren't Michelin-star meals, but you know ... I still grew pretty tall.

Do you have credit card debt? Don't pay them off late. Penalty fees are the most infuriating, useless expenses ever. Pay credit card debt first. You must pay off your credit card debt anyway. Better do it with the smallest possible cost.

Write down every expense that you have in a month-long period. Everything, even down to the last toilet paper roll. At the end of the month, go through your household and find the items you didn't necessarily need.

Look over your list and see where you can cut out some expenses. Maybe go down on your cable package or switch cell phone companies. Any way you can save money, do it. When you find the amount of money you didn't need to spend in the month, put that number as your target savings for the next month.

Realize that all five of these money myths are just that — they are myths! You don't need to believe them or buy into their lies. These myths are not healthy or helpful and will only harm your future wealth. In the next few chapters, we will discuss how you can budget and accumulate your savings by avoiding the common financial mistakes many individuals make.

Chapter 2: The debt epidemic

Right now, I can tell you exactly what the mathematical formula for Pythagorean Theorem is. It's $a^2 + b^2 = c^2$. That is how you find a bunch of different measurements for triangles.

Now let me ask you this: How many times have you used Pythagorean Theorem since you graduated your high school math class? I can bet that you have used it less than five times — including helping your child with their homework. And yet, that formula was drilled into my mind day after day throughout math class. Why? Who knows! But you know what I didn't learn in class? Why I shouldn't be buying my tenth pair of Nikes or my hundredth shade of Mac lipstick.

I didn't learn how to do my taxes, how to manage my money, or what debt is. School taught me none of the "real life" stuff.

So, there I was, working, studying, and wondering how I could afford the lifestyle I wanted. So I started taking some financial classes at the university for extra credit. I hoped they would help me understand my situation. When I took them, I learned various economic and financial terms, I learned about the stock market, but I still learned nothing about why I shouldn't be eating out every night.

School won't teach you real-life finances. You can buy the upsold product of some finance guru for thousands of dollars. They will teach you how to be rich at the age of fifty for a price that requires you to mortgage your home. There you might learn real-life finances. However, to simply learn to manage your money, you don't need to go to those lengths.

People hate talking about debt. Some people say do not ever get into debt, others say take a risk and go into debt for a larger profit. Who can you believe these days? I get it, maybe you are knee-deep in debt and want out. Maybe you are thinking of going into debt and looking for guidance. We all get there at some point in life.

But before we make that decision, we hear a small whisper in our ear telling us various items of advice. And guess what? Oftentimes, that advice sucks. I hate to say it, but that angel on your shoulder isn't all that smart. Turns out that small voice is really what we have learned in the past and merely believe to be good advice.

You Are Not Your Parents

Growing up, I constantly heard my grandparents talk about money. Talking is a generous term; most times, it was arguing — loud arguing. Even though they had some money, there seemed to never be enough. It drilled into my mind that money is bad. Money is a necessary evil, and the only way you get enough of it is to lie and cheat yourself into becoming rich.

I was told the best way to live your life is to go to school, get a mediocre-paying job, invest in a 401k and a home, and retire when you are 65. Along this path, I would pick up debt from student loans and buy a home. But this was good debt, my teachers said. And I believed them.

This mindset is what has led to the modern debt epidemic. We pull out debt after debt because we think it's good, that it will help us. It is good to have "free money" and satisfy wishes quickly. But it backfires bitterly.

If you are in debt, you aren't alone. In fact, corporations also go into debt. A few notable companies are Lehman Brothers, AIG, and General Motors. All of these companies went into debt because they handled their money poorly. Bad financial decisions and money mismanagement is quite frequently a problem among companies, too, not just individuals.

A Short History of Debt

The US has had financial problems for the past 100 years, and the roaring monster who is responsible for most of these financial problems is known as Mr. Debt.

Debt started accumulating in crazy numbers in the aftermath of World War II. After the war, the housing market boomed and FHA mortgages were newly available. The debt was wrapped up in a big box with a pretty bow and made to look like what every American household should be.

People were then scrambling to buy a house and pull out enough debt to secure the house. They called these loans "easy debt" to make them sound desirable and fancy. People loved it! Your average person started accumulating debt big-time.

This led to the states printing more money without enough coverage, and this balloon of uncovered financial aid grew bigger and bigger until ... POP! 2008 came and the recession hit.

While this is a main source of our financial crisis, personal debt dates back even farther than the wars. It even predates the existence of money, per se. In the ancient times when people didn't have enough goods to offer in exchange for other goods, they often offered their work for food and other necessities. This often resulted in self-inflicted slavery. The rudimentary form of debt was physically horrifying. Today, stress coming from debt leaves mental marks. The origin is still the same — people spending more than they can afford.

Where is all this debt coming from? Personal debt is every credit card balance that goes unpaid, every loan taken out, and anything else you spent creditors' money on.

Why do so many of us find ourselves in debt? The reality of finding ourselves in the financial crisis is that our monthly income is not enough to afford our lifestyle. You might be thinking to yourself, "But I don't live a luxurious lifestyle!" That's probably true.

However, even non-luxurious lifestyles can still create debt. Debt happens whenever your spending exceeds your income.

The problem occurs because you spend money you do not have. On top of this, the creditors lend you money that they don't have, and then they charge you interest on this loan, expecting you to somehow come up with money that doesn't even exist. There is actually more debt in the world than there is money to cover this debt. Society at large is playing a giant game of musical chairs.

Around and around debt goes, trying to grab those money chairs. When the music finally stops, everyone sits down as quick as they can! But there's always one person left out. This person gets eaten alive by debts. Figuratively, of course.

Since there is not enough money to cover the debt, you can imagine that the interest is a non-existent amount as well. Following this logic, there will always be people who won't be able to pay off their debt plus the interest. There is always a sum of debt that is unable to be paid off. It sounds crazy, right?

The debt crisis is partially due to the fact that people aren't being paid more. Our incomes are the same as they were in the 1980s. When someone gets a raise, it is just counterbalancing with inflation. And in fact, people are sometimes getting paid even less now than they were back in the 80s (once you adjust for inflation).

Think of it like this: In the 1980s, maybe a copywriter made $5 a day. Bread only cost $0.50 a loaf. Easy to afford! Now, this same copywriter makes $25 a day, but bread now costs $3.00 a loaf. Before, a copywriter could buy ten loaves of bread from a day's wage. Today, he can only buy eight.

When adjusted for inflation, the copywriter now makes less than the copywriter in the 80s because the cost of goods and living have gone up so much. Since the buying power of wages didn't increase, neither did economic growth, and finally, the bubble popped.

But even though the cost of living and goods have gone up, we should still be able to afford to live. So why do so many of us find ourselves armpit-deep in debt?

Because the choice of goods increased significantly. There are more options of what to buy today. We also have a new power called marketing that makes us believe that we need every new gadget and we need it now, otherwise we're lame, unfashionable, and so on. Most people, however, don't make nearly as much as they would need to in order to keep up with the trends. So what do they do?

Do they wear the same pair of jeans and use the same car for ten years ...?

Nope. They engage in debt.

The most popular forms of debt are credit card debt, student loans, auto loans, mortgages, and home equity line of credit. If you do not have any type of debt, keep up this good habit. But if you are like how I was, or like the average American, you have at least one of these types of debt.

None of these debts start out with bad intentions. You think to yourself that you need to go to school, you have to buy a car, you need groceries, you need a house, and come up with a ton of other reasons.

No one sets out to get themselves into debt. We have been warned about debt our whole lives, but we are also told that if we do not have a good credit score, we'll never be able to buy anything. And how do you get a good credit score? Racking up debt and paying it off within the allotted time.

Sound backwards? It is! Think of credit cards. You use them to buy everything you need, like groceries and gas. You look at your statement at the end of the month and it's way more than you thought. It's easier to spend the money when you don't have to fish it out of your purse. And so those bills go unpaid.

Credit card debt is highest among people in their sixties and seventies, but student loans and auto loans are highest among people in their twenties and thirties. This shows that most people struggle with debt, but different debts plague different age groups.

It is easily noted that debt causes stress. You know when your friend pays for your lunch and you feel the immediate need to pay them back? That's how debt feels too! It causes everyone stress.

But some debt may be unavoidable in short-term circumstances. What do you think about debt? Do you think it is necessary to survive? Or do you avoid it like the plague? There may even be some things you feel like you could go into debt for.

What Will You Go Into Debt For?

Think of what matters to you. Think of what you want your successful life to look like. Now think of things you believe are worthy to go into debt for. Grab a sheet of paper and a pen.

Write down the top five most important things in your life and how those items could lead to a level of debt you would be comfortable with.

For example, if your top priority is family, you may be comfortable going into debt to get a mortgage to have your family in a safe and stable environment. If your dream is to become a professor, you may be comfortable pulling out student loans.

After you write this list, write down everything you spend your money on. How much do these lists overlap? If you spend money on cable, getting your nails done, and going out to eat, but you only feel comfortable going into debt for student loans, those lists do not overlap at all.

Oftentimes, we find that our lists don't overlap much. This is because our brains are hard-wired to work on a short-term reward system.

When you reward yourself, your brain releases dopamine and you get excited. That's why you love to buy those new shoes or devour a piece of chocolate cake.

Our brains make us believe that we need these daily indulgences, when in reality, we don't! This short-term gratification doesn't lead to lasting happiness, but instead leads to more debt. Often, it's not even the debt we'd consider worth "dying" for.

No matter what your reasons are for going into debt, you have to be careful. Debt can sweep the rug out from under your feet before you can realize it. One day you're only $100 in debt, and the next, you wake up drowning in thousands of dollars of debt.

Every time you contemplate going into debt, you must think about whether or not it is worth it in the long run. To stay afloat, get out of debt, and live the life you want, you must have a good financial planning system in place. You have to resist the urge to buy today at tomorrow's expense.

When you purchase things on credit, it can be hard to not go into debt. In the next few chapters, we will go over everything you need to plan out your financial future so you can get out of debt and become financially stable.

Chapter 3: Budgeting Essentials

Before building a budget, there are a few things you should look into so you understand your budgeting needs better. First, let's see what a financial blueprint is.

According to Wealth Advisors, LLC, "a financial blueprint is a comprehensive financial plan: It spells out the financial means and methods for accomplishing your specific goals. It is a comprehensive and coordinated approach to personal financial decision-making. It is an ongoing process that requires monitoring to help ensure that your objectives and goals are met."[i]

To put it simply, look at where you are now, plan for where you want to be tomorrow, and take into consideration that these two data points create a long-term financial plan for yourself.

You might think, "Oh, that's so simple. I bet everybody is doing it." You would be wrong. Even though it is indeed simple to create a budget to cover your personal finances, less people do it than you'd imagine. According to the National Association of Personal Financial Advisors, almost 60% of US adults don't have any financial plan. NAPFA also shows that 39% of US adults don't have any other type of savings than pensions. 50% of Americans with children don't have a will, and two out of five Americans would give Cs, Ds, or Fs to their level of financial awareness.[ii]

"Failing to plan is planning to fail."

What does it mean to have a financial plan? How does it benefit you?

First of all, a financial planner offers you transparency. Planning your life goals and desires financially will help you see the big picture of how and when you can achieve them. You'll also have clear knowledge about your daily, monthly, and yearly expenditures.

You'll be able to see how and where you can cut expenses to regroup your money for a better cause. By analyzing your spending habits, you can develop a realistic budget that you can stick to. You'll cultivate trust and respect toward yourself when you see the first fruits of your financial resilience.

You can always turn to a professional financial planner to help you map out your finances. A professional will be able to determine your net worth, give you information about life planning assumptions like inflation rates, rate of return, saving ratios, etc. If you're thinking about investing, a professional can help you find the opportunities that best fit your needs (low-risk, high-interest).

Be cautious on who you choose to be your financial advisor, though. Don't buy into every "just now, just for you" deals.

Moreover, having a financial advisor doesn't mean you can take your hands off your financial self-education. You should always be aware of what's happening with your money and understand the process you get yourself into. An advisor is merely a tutor who helps you find the best solutions. You have to learn the lessons, nevertheless.

I know, learning real-life finances by yourself is tough. You may wonder — just like I did — why didn't they teach me this in school? The question is legit. Our education failed in preparing us to handle our financial adulthood. According to Money Savvy Youth, only 59% percent of young adults pay their bills on time. 81% of college students underestimate the time they could pay off their student loans in.[iii] 76% of families live paycheck to paycheck, and 27% have zero savings.[iv]

When it comes to financial awareness, there is no difference between our parents' generation and us. Our education system still doesn't care about improving these crazy statistics. It is not surprising that our financial awareness turned out to be as bad as our parents' — that's what we learned. But it is up to us now to improve the knowledge we lack individually. Schools supposedly teach us how to make good money, but they never teach how to manage it. If you want to be financially (care) free, you have to learn it for yourself.

Your financial goals

Financial goals can be anything from buying a new phone to achieving financial freedom. Not everybody aims to be a millionaire. It is not easy to become one — definitely not as easy as some "gurus" may present it. Some people value other stuff more than money. There's nothing wrong with that. But let's face it, regardless of where our values lie, we can explore them much better if we have money. Or at least financial security.

Do you have a charitable heart? You can help more buying food for ten than preparing food for one.

Do you love spending time with your family? Well, guess what buys you time?

Your financial goals don't have to be strictly money-related. Do you want a weekend at the seaside with your family? Do you crave a new computer? Do you want to improve your presentation skills with a course? Plan out their financial path.

Many people who try budgeting get off track by setting unrealistic goals. For example, saving for a private jet is not the most realistic goal to have, even if you make around $100,000 a year. To be able to create realistic and achievable goals, you need to examine two things:

- your income
- your expenses

Income:

Income is your monthly salary, your passive income stream (royalties, interests, shares, etc.), bonuses, inheritance, or winnings. Everything that adds money to your tab is income.

Expenses:

Everything that takes away from your tab is an expense. I separate three types of expenses.

Essentials: food, housing-related costs, utility bills, and transportation. I consider phone and Internet bills essential in the age we're living in. Feel free to exclude them from your essentials list if you disagree. Some people do.

Personal expenses: cable TV bills, coffee breaks in a café, makeup, clothing, gym memberships, dining out, other memberships … I consider extra luxury choices in your essentials to also be a personal expense. For example, if you rent an apartment in the city center, that by itself is not a luxury. If you rent the rooftop apartment for better view with an extra 10% rental fee, that's a luxury.

Savings (or the "get ahead" category). Having savings can grant you a feeling of safety. You can be sure that if a car hits you, if you fall ill, or if you just need to fly to the aid of a distant relative at the last minute, money won't be a problem. The most common expenses in the "savings" category are: savings plans, emergency funds, debt payments, and retirement savings.

Take some time to write a list about your income and expenses. You can take a piece of paper and divide it into two columns. One column stands for income, the other for expenses. You must know the exact number of fixed expenses like subscription fees, membership fees, and utility bills. If you don't know the exact amount you spend on food, for example, just estimate a number. Next month, I promise you'll know that number to the last cent. Add together the two columns.

Check which side of the balance is bigger, the income or expenses. If it's the expenses, that's a problem, especially if they don't include any savings. If about 20% of your expenses go to savings, you're on board. If not, your options are to either increase your income (harder) or cut your expenses (easier). To make it easier, shift your mindset about the *income – expenses = savings* equation to *income – savings = expenses.*

Do you want to accumulate savings for a car, house, or just in general? Do you have any debts to pay off? If you answered yes to either of these questions, you're in the desperate need of a budget.

Budgeting is not easy. It involves painful compromises, difficult choices, and many renunciations. However, as long as your goals are realistic, the effort will be worthwhile. Some scammy books will tell that you can achieve everything you want financially, as long as you follow their scammy advice. Well, if that were true, by now there should have been an alarming increase in the population of millionaires.

Of course, you can and should aim to make more money. But first, you should learn to handle what you have now. More money won't help you be better with money.

Set SMART goals

SMART is an abbreviation for Specific, Measurable, Achievable, Relevant, and Time-framed. Your financial goals should be inserted in the SMART framework. Make sure your financial goals have a specific dollar amount and a deadline assigned to them. Come up with an example of a goal and lead it through these five aspects.

For example, if you want to take a two-week trip to Europe to celebrate your tenth marriage anniversary, how could this trip be achieved?

Let's say you've looked into dates, flights, accommodations, and it would cost $3000. You want to go next year — in twelve months. This means that you have twelve months to save

$3000. This means you have to save $250/month. Do you find saving this amount realistic? Can you spare this money?

If not, you have to reevaluate the goal, the deadline, or the budget. Whether you start to save earlier, whether you change the destination, it's up to you. If you do find saving that amount to be realistic for you, congratulations! You just set a SMART goal.

The goal is specific: a two-week trip to Europe. It is measurable: $3000. If you can save $250 a month, it means the goal is achievable. It is also relevant. You don't have a ten-year marriage anniversary every day, after all. Finally, the goal is time-framed — next year.

Good luck.

Chapter 4: Getting Out of Debt

I already mentioned that when I was a student, my income was around $200 a month. This was hard to live on, and when I found myself wanting a new computer, I decided to pull out a student loan for $1000. Even if I'd dedicated all of my monthly income to pay off this student loan, it would have taken me five whole months to pay off. But I was desperate, and my mind fixated on this computer.

Literally the day after I applied for the student loan, my uncle gave me a computer as a gift. I was overjoyed! But guess what I didn't do? I didn't return the $1000 student loan. Nope, instead I spent every last penny. And did I spend it on good things? Not exactly.

I took that thousand dollars and bought new clothes, teeth whitening treatments, and Christmas gifts. The key takeaway here is *never apply for a loan.* But if you must, don't do it around the holidays. At the time, taking the student loan did not seem like a bad idea, but as soon as I started to pay it off, I regretted bitterly. $1000 quickly became $1500, and I realized how stupid my choice was.

I had to learn my lesson the hard way. But at least I did. And let's face it, the amount could have been worse. For many, it is. I decided to set out to inform and teach others to not make the same mistakes. If you are not currently in debt, do not get in it.

If I could turn back time, I would never have applied for the student loan. Even for the computer, I would not have gotten it. Knowing what I know now, I would have saved my money and purchased that computer at a later time. I paid more than $500 to the bank due to interest. I got nothing on that money — no goods, no happiness, only the vague joy of buying useless stuff quicker than usual.

The best way to get out of debt — quickly

Don't wait. As soon as you can, start paying off any loan that you have. When you wait and the interest accumulates, it is much more difficult to pay off that loan.

Let's say you have a loan that you pay $100 to every single month. When your monthly check comes in and you made $500, don't think that. Instead, think that you made $400 because you already know that $100 is going straight to the loan. This little psychological trick can help you to stick to your budget. You do not have $500 a month to spend because that $100 is not yours. Recognize that whatever is paid to loans is not part of your income. You can't escape it. Death, taxes, and debt collectors will always find you.

Pay your debts off quickly, starting with the ones with the *highest interest rates.*

Credit-card-free through college

If you are currently a college student, try to avoid credit cards. A college education does not guarantee that you are going to know how to manage your finances. With the sky-high prices of tuition these days, it is best to not get into more debt than you need to. That means avoiding those credit cards. You won't have a stable income (probably), so you can easily end up spending more than you can afford when it doesn't need to be paid off until the end of the month. That is how many people end up in debt way too early. School won't teach you how to use your credit card wisely, anyway.

It's better that you don't spend more than you can safely afford. Your credit score is important and can be detrimental to your future if you ruin it in your youth.

Have a Good FICO Score

It is important for you to have a good FICO credit score. The FICO score is "a credit score in the United States that represents the credit worthiness of a person, the likelihood that person will pay his or her debts." Many institutions will use this credit score to evaluate their risk when they lend you money. Banks and credit card companies will use this number to decide how much they can safely lend to you. A widespread use of credit scores has made credit easier to attain for many consumers.

The FICO score is the most widely used measurement for "repayment ability" and ranges from 300 to 850. If you have a credit score of 750 to 850, then the risk of lending to you is fairly low. This is considered an excellent score, and if you fall into this range, then you will have access to the lowest rates and best loan terms.

If you are wondering how you get your credit score, you're not alone. Data from your credit report gets put into five major categories that make up your FICO score. The scoring model applies different weights to different categories.

For example, 35% of your score is made up of your payment history and whether you always pay off your balance or if you are often late. 30% of your credit score is how much you owe on different loans or credit cards, 15% is comprised of how long your credit has been accumulating, 10% is made up of new credit, and the remaining 10% is affected by the types of credit cards you use. So as you can see, there are lots of different factors here. The most important is how you pay your bills. If you pay your bills and don't let them gather interest, you are more likely to have a better FICO score.[v]

How Can You Get Rid of Your Debt?

Many people nowadays find themselves stuck in the debt epidemic. Know you are not alone. Sometimes it may seem like you are so deeply in debt that there is no way out. There is always a way. But to turn the debt-ship around takes time, patience, and yes, renunciation.

1. Stop Creating More Debt

This one may seem obvious, but I still have to say it. The first step to getting rid of your debt is to stop creating more debt. Stop purchasing more stuff. Even if you have a few "extra" dollars in the bank, it doesn't mean you should purchase something else. Just because you might be able to buy it doesn't mean you should.

Lots of people have a hard time saying no. If you find yourself unable to stop purchasing things, reevaluate your goals. Ask yourself what makes you happy. Is it acquiring more things? I bet this does not give you a lot of happiness. If buying things does make you happy, it is short-term happiness. What will make you happier, more stuff or financial peace of mind?

2. Rank Your Debts

The second step in getting out of debt is running inventory on your debts and then rank them in order of urgency. *The debt with the highest interest rate is your most urgent one.* For example, if you have credit card debt, always pay this one off first. Credit cards have notoriously high-interest rates of 18-22% or more. Credit card debt will literally cripple your finances.

As long as you have credit card debt, you are essentially stealing money from your own purse. Don't even think about paying off another debt before this one. If you have $5,000 in credit card debt at a 20% interest rate, then you are going to be paying a lot of money. Let's say you pay the minimum payment of $100 a month. Your debt won't be paid for over nine years. And to make matters worse, you will actually end up paying $10,840 due to the additional $5,840 interest you accumulated over those years. Is it worth it?

3. Get a Lower Interest Rate

If you know that paying off your debts will take some time, the best thing you can do for yourself is to try and get a lower interest rate. One way to lower your credit card debt, for example, is to do a balance transfer.

A balance transfer is when you move your credit card balance to another bank. The other bank will do this for you because they want your business, so they are going to give you a lower interest rate. You can shop around at different banks and companies to find the lowest interest rate available.

Try looking for one that keeps a low and steady interest rate throughout the debt. Some banks will have interest rates that raise after a few months or a year. When you do the balance transfer, always double-check the terms and conditions. You don't want to move your balance to another bank only to find that it is worse than the first one. The devil always lies in the fine print.

4. Go Through Your Expenses

In the previous chapter, I talked about writing down every expense for a month. Grab that paper again. Look at your expenses and rate them in order of importance and urgency. Your debt repayment should be the first one on your list. Go through the expenses and try to find any that you might be able to cut out.

For example, if you treat yourself on the daily to store-bought coffee, try cutting that out completely or only doing it once a week (I know, I always mention coffee as the deterring example. I'm a writer; coffee is my greatest expense. Please forgive me for my biased example). These less important expenses are easy to cut out. Just think about how important your debt repayment is. If you don't pay your debt off in time, you can incur crazy expensive fees which add up quickly.

5. Schedule Your Repayment

Getting out of debt is as easy as paying off what you owe. However, with a limited income, that can be hard. The loans seem to get bigger and bigger, and you can feel like you are at a loss for what to do. Once you decide what expenses you can cut out and how much money you can put toward your debt each month, map out how long it will take for you to pay off your debt.

For example, maybe you are able to pay $300 toward your debt a month. Let's say you have credit card debt of $500 and then a student loan of $1,000. You will put the $300 toward your credit card payment for two months until it is paid off because that's the highest interest rate. Once that is paid off, you roll over your payments into your student loan payment.

So for the next four months, you will pay the whole $300 to your student loan payment. Each time you pay off a debt, roll that money into paying off the next debt. When you are 100% debt-free, save that money each month to create a good savings or investment account.

6. Create Multiple Income Streams

If you ever talk to a successful and wealthy individual, they will tell you that you have to have multiple streams of income. Your nine-to-five job just won't cut it if you want to be financially free. The Internet has created an abundance of opportunities for you to make some side cash.

This can be as easy as walking your neighbor's dogs, doing yardwork, or working completely online. You can learn the tricks and trades of penny stocks if you have some extra money, or you can work on freelance websites using skills that you already have.

Sites like Fiverr and Upwork are easy enough to sign up for and make money from in your spare time. If you have any skills like writing, you can find jobs writing on Upwork. You can become a personal assistant, cover designer, or even find freelance IT jobs. The options are almost unlimited. Where there is a will, there is a way. Becoming a freelancer (even if only part-time) is an easy way to make money without investing your hard-earned income.

If you want to be successful on freelance sites, don't hesitate to put yourself out there. Apply for the jobs that excite you and challenge you. Not only will you get to learn something new, but it can create lasting relationships with clients who will use your service again.

Once your debt is fully paid off, commit to being financially responsible. You must change your financial attitude to avoid getting into debt again at all costs. When you get into debt, you find yourself in a well that is very hard to dig out of.

Debt comes at a high price, one you should not be comfortable paying. The next chapter will talk about how you can spend less and why you might even become happier by doing it.

Chapter 5: Spend Less

As the old saying goes, "Money can't buy happiness." This is true, to an extent. Money is not bad. You will not be unhappy because you have money, just like you won't be happy because you don't have money. Happiness comes from within; it is something we create.

But we all seem to have a problem with this creation. Most people these days think that money, in fact, does equal happiness. They find themselves purchasing that new pair of shoes or that third watch because buying things makes them feel good. It creates temporary happiness. If you are not happy being poor, you will not be happy being rich. The ability of appreciating what we have is the same when you have little and when you have more.

More stuff will not make you happier. In fact, excess and clutter around your house will harm your productivity levels and make you even unhappier! A good life is not determined by the items in your home. It is determined by who you are and who you spend your life with. This is why it is important to not base your happiness on the money you are spending.

Spending wisely and less will make you happier in the long run. You will not have to precariously walk through your house that is filled with the endless amount of items you have bought and never used. Waste is going to cause you stress, especially if it pairs up with lack of money, or with debt hanging above your head.

A house filled with clutter is a mind filled with clutter. Even in your peaceful times, you'll have to brainstorm about where you can put this and that to have a space to do yoga in, for example. Clutter is stressful, ugly, and completely unnecessary. You will have to spend more time cleaning everything, and let's be honest, no one likes cleaning.

Overspending wreaks havoc on your finances. It steals away your peace of mind by throwing you into debt. Overspending is a cunning monster. It comes to you wrapped in a ribbon and bow and looks like cool new products you have to have. But once you buy these new items, you realize you have been tricked into debt once again.

Most people could spend less. They find themselves spending more money than they need to because they get carried away when they see advertisements. These advertisements trick them into thinking that if they buy the product listed, they will be happier, sexier, funnier, etc. Well, guess what? It is all a scam. These advertisements will not make you happier, sexier, or funnier. Just poorer. So one way to spend less is to avoid advertisements.

How Can You Avoid Ads?

If you want to avoid ads, you first need to understand how they work. If you recognize their gimmicks, they lot easier to ignore and not buy into. Ads are pretty easy to decipher. Their tricks are straightforward and often pushed into our faces.

For example, think of toothpaste commercials. Toothpaste commercials are filled with attractive people that have straight and white teeth. They are depicted as sexy and socially admired. When you see these toothpaste commercials, you hear about the great benefits of the brand, how it helps to keep your teeth healthy, and how it will whiten your pearly whites. But what is left unsaid?

When you view a toothpaste commercial, your mind thinks that by using the product, you will be socially admired, respected, loved, and to top it all off, you are going to have straight and white teeth! Ah, if only it were that easy.

The common theme in ads is to make the viewer feel good. Ads touch on your ego to make you want to be better. Ads that are especially popular feature celebrity testimonials and "honest" reviews of product testers to achieve their "life-changing results." If Jennifer Aniston used it, it can't be bad, right?

Advertisers play on the fact that an average person reviewing the product will relate the most to you. When this average person shows up on your screen, you feel like you can trust this individual since they are one of us. Your brain relates to the commercial character and you see yourself in them. Whether the product is great or not, this stage of the commercial is meant to impress you and get you to buy it.

The next time you see an ad, question whether what they are using and doing is real. Think of a haircare commercial. When they say their hair is shiny and beautiful just from washing it with the advertised shampoo, what are you thinking? Does hair really look like that just from washing it? No, it doesn't. Remind yourself that five hairdressers worked on that woman's hair and added 300 grams of extensions to get it to look like that. Or think of that cool car commercial that makes the driver look sexy and mysterious. Ask yourself:

"Will a car make me more attractive?"

Even if it did, would you want to be with someone who liked you just for your car?

When you ask yourself these questions, the effects that ads rely on can be turned off quite easily. But that's not all advertisements strive to do to you. Advertising has actually changed over the years. In the early period of modern advertising, there were two separate products. These were long-term purchases and perishables.

Long-term purchases were items like cars, houses, electronic tools, and long-lasting clothing like jeans. Perishables included any item that would be of short-term use like food, lingerie, and cosmetics. Today's advertising market tries to make you look at long-term purchases as short-term purchases.

This is why advertisers try so hard to get you to buy a new car every year. Your two-year-old car is not bad. Seriously, my grandpa drove the same Lada for 40 years! Like the old saying goes, if it's not broke, don't fix it! But in today's world, we think that we need the new item. This is how companies thrive and create their business. They profit off of our financial ignorance.

Advertisers no longer focus on the future benefits of products. Instead, they focus on promising to take away a current problem you have. *Now. Immediately. Instantly*. Need to lose a few pounds? Try this weight-loss supplement. Hate your teeth? Try that new toothpaste. Want to look rich? Buy a new car!

Ads catch you in your pain of the moment. It is much easier to recall and relate with your current pain than it is to imagine future happiness. You'd rather have the solution to your pain now, quickly, instead of putting a lot of time and effort to have it later. Because of this, advertisements try to feed on your pain points.

Don't buy into these tricks. Buying a cheaper coffee at Starbucks saves you a few bucks daily, but it isn't going to make you rich. To build up real wealth, you have to save money on the big purchases like cars, smart phones, and other electronics. This means distinguishing the real perishable items in your life from the long-term purchases. Your old items will continue to work and last a lot longer than those advertisers try to make you believe. Unless you are getting tax benefits from these purchases, resist the urge to make them.

Another way to stop buying into ads is to be aware of online advertisements. Resist the urge to subscribe to websites, and use ad blockers. When you subscribe to different sites, they will email you about sales and other promotions they are having. And like I talked about earlier, just because something is on sale doesn't mean you should be buying it.

You can also set up an expense limit on ads. Once a week, you buy something silly, unnecessary, or random to satisfy your cravings, but anything that costs more than a dollar, or five dollars, you automatically ignore. This way, you can allow a little indulgence in your life, but you won't overspend your budget. For example, buying a book that you feel would help you for a dollar or five dollars is a good investment. Or if your favorite mascara is discounted to four dollars at Nordstrom Rack, it is better to buy it now than when it will be eight again. Unless you just bought a mascara; then it's better to save those bucks for something better. Something's six bucks? Forget about it. I know, it's just a dollar difference — but that doesn't matter. You have to draw a line somewhere for your indulgence expenses. If you don't respect your own boundaries, who will?

Many of us struggle with trying to keep up with the Joneses. We buy things we don't need just because we see other people have them. I hate to break it to you, but people don't care about what you have nearly as much as you think they do. If you try to impress people with the stuff you buy, you will only earn their envy, not their admiration. This, in turn, will not make you any happier.

Instead of collecting objects, try to collect memories. Save up your money and spend it making memories. These fun experiences will last a lot longer in your mind than the things you can buy. Short-term satisfaction may come from purchases, but long-term happiness comes from the people you surround yourself with and the experiences you partake in.

Think of it like this: Do you remember your first day of high school or college? Probably. Do you remember what you were wearing? Probably not. Just like you will remember your first time camping or skydiving, you will remember future experiences. No one remembers the fifth vase they bought that year.

Quick Tips to Save Money:

Getting out of debt starts with learning to save your money. If you think that's impossible, you don't know what I'm about to tell you.

First of all, learn to buy in bulk. You save much more money by buying family-sized items and portioning them out, rather than buying individual-sized servings. For example, buy a tub of yogurt instead of the individual servings. While the individuals may be convenient, you will save money by buying the bigger size.

Also, try your hand at couponing. You don't need to go extreme. If you are already going to purchase the item, look online or in newspaper ads for a coupon to help you save. However, don't buy an item simply because you have a coupon. This takes you back into the spending mindset. The correct thought process is, "I want to buy this and that, so I will look for a coupon," not, "I have this coupon, so now I have to go to buy this and that to take advantage of a good deal." It is never a good deal when you buy something for the sake of its price and not for the sake of its utility.

Avoid impulse buying. Look at each item and ask yourself how often you will use it and if you really need it. Don't go to shopping malls unless you have a specific item you need.

Never grocery shop while you're hungry! I think you know what I mean. When you're hungry, you overestimate your need for food and you'll end up buying much more than you need. You'll also be in a hurry with a clouded brain focused on nothing but eating. You will end up buying a lot more than you want, need, or can afford. Better have a quick snack before going to the supermarket. Snacks also cost money, but overall, your balance will still be better.

Did you know that keeping your chargers and other cords plugged into the wall takes energy, even if you are not currently using the item? Of course you know. But did you know that 5-10% of your energy bill might come from appliances left on standby? Add up how much your energy bill is each month in a year. Got the result? What's 10% of that? One hundred bucks? Two hundred? When you leave the house, unplug your items. Close your windows as well to save on your cold or warm air escaping. These are small victories, but if each penny matters to you, then take this small step to save. It doesn't really cost you anything — not even time. Think about it as getting paid for doing nothing.

One of the biggest steps you can take to save money is to eat and cook at home. Eating out at fast food restaurants can cost you thousands of dollars a year. You can never know what is in a meal unless you've made it yourself. The calories add up too. Before you know it, you'll start spending on expensive weight-loss programs, supplements, and whatnot. By cooking your food at home, you will not only save a ton of money, but you'll also be healthier.

While these quick tips can help you save some extra cash, the next chapter will talk about how you can build your savings account and turn your finances around for the better.

Chapter 6: Savings

The one financial goal almost everyone can agree on is that you should have money put aside into savings. When you are struggling on a daily basis to pay your bills, a savings account seems about as realistic as a unicorn. You might be thinking, *How am I supposed to save money when I can't even pay my bills?* It's truly a problem many people are struggling with in this day and age.

But even if you are currently stuck in debt, planning on opening a savings account is an important step to have to wait on you as you crawl your way out. It may seem unrealistic, but I'm about to show you just how you can make pigs fly and start gathering savings while still in debt.

Important notice: When I talk about debt here, I mean low-interest-rate debt. As long as you have high-interest-rate debts, you'd better focus all your financial power to get rid of those. When, however, you reach a point where you debt has low interest, you can repay it with the monthly minimum amount and put a little money aside to a savings account. I warn you, this account won't be an inexhaustible pot of gold, especially while you struggle with debt. But for the sake of financial awareness, practice, and improvement, it is better to have it.

Before you can start drafting up your savings, you need to know where you stand. Take inventory of your life. Looking at where you currently are is key to understanding where you are going. If you are lost, how can you get back to where you need to be? Think of your cell phone's GPS. Thankfully, we are never lost very long with our trusty smart phones, but in order for our maps app to work, it has to find our location and then route directions to the nearest destination.

Getting out of debt is pretty similar to your phone giving you directions. If you know your destination, great! But if you don't know your current location, you won't be routed to your destination, so we need to start by taking inventory of your debt.

Look over all of your bank statements, credit card statements, loans, and any savings you might have. Write down the main figures and then take a step back. This needs to be looked at from the big picture. If you have double the debt compared to the money you have coming in, it is unrealistic to save a large percentage of your income. Or any, really. As I mentioned before, settle on paying the high-interest debt off first. Estimate how much time would this take with your current income. Don't try to get clever assuming that in two months you'll get back some money from Jack, and Jane will finally pay you for the VHS player you gave her in advance. Only count on what's certain. Anything unexpected is just a bonus.

You need to know how much money you have coming in and how much money you have going out on a monthly basis so you can decide how much your income will allow you to save. Estimate how long it will take you to open a savings account. If based on your current situation it will take you months or even a year, do your homework about savings account options. Which are the best institutions to put your savings in?

Which have the lowest fees, highest interest rates, etc.?

When you're finally debt-free

You will hear a lot of financial experts say that you need to pay yourself first. If you don't own your own business, you probably think paying yourself seems a little counterintuitive. But what this actually means is that every time you get a paycheck, you set aside a percentage of your income to go into savings before you pay those bills.

"Paying" yourself allows you to build your savings before the money disappears in the chasm of bills. It is recommended that you save 10% of your income, so a dime for every dollar. That doesn't seem too bad, right? Well, I understand that it may still be unrealistic for someone on a very tight budget. Therefore, start saving whatever you can. Even if you only pay yourself a penny on the dollar, it is still savings.

Always keep your savings goal realistic. Let's say that you want to build a $1,200 emergency fund.

Not a bad goal to start with. If you make $3,000 a month once taxes are taken out, it will take you four months to build that emergency fund if you save 10%.

It is important to have a goal in mind. If you know the exact amount you want to save, you can work backward and determine how many months it will take you to save that money. Having this goal in place allows you to remember why you are doing the saving process in the first place and holds you accountable to actually put that money into savings.

While putting aside money for savings is always important, you don't want to be eating Top Ramen for every meal. Put aside a realistic amount that you can save every month so that you aren't skimping on necessary items like food and electricity. Like I mentioned earlier, even if it is only a penny on the dollar, it's still a penny!

Types of Saving Methods You Can Use

One of the most obvious ways to put aside money into savings is in a traditional savings account. In fact, you probably already have one set up at your bank. Traditional savings accounts can be easy and convenient, since they are usually attached to the checking account your income already goes into. This way, you can easily move the money over into your savings as soon as you get paid.

However, even though they can be convenient, they may not be the best option if you are looking to gain interest. Traditional savings accounts usually only gain about .2-.5% in interest every year. A lot of savings accounts also ask for a minimum account balance to keep monthly fees away. This can be troublesome for you if you don't have a few hundred dollars to open the account or a continuous, stable amount of money you can add to the account each month.

One perk of having a savings account with your current bank is that you can withdraw from it at any time. While this is obviously not the goal, if you are saving for an emergency fund, this is probably the best choice.

Nowadays, you can even have an online savings account. These only need a deposit as little as one dollar at some institutions, so it is a great option for those who don't have money rolling in to save.

They also gain more interest than your traditional savings at 1-2%. They are still government insured, and you can transfer money all online.

If you don't want to open a savings account, you can put aside your money into a certificate of deposit or a share certificate. Most of these require at least $500 to use. Their interest is around 1-2% and can be found at any bank or credit union. While the money is available for immediate withdrawal, there is an interest penalty. This can be good for people who may be tempted to pull their money out of their savings. You know that if you pull it out, you will suffer a penalty on your interest gained.

If you are tempted to use your savings like your checking, you can put your savings into U.S. savings bonds. These only require a deposit as low as $25 and then are locked for 12 months. These garner around 1.5% interest, making them the better choice when compared to a traditional savings account.

Your last option for where to deposit your savings would be a money market account. Money market accounts need around $250 to open and gain .1-.3% interest. While this may be the lowest interest-earning option, you do not have to worry about bank fees or minimum transactions or balances one you have the account. The access to funds is immediate and you don't lose out on interest or pay a fee for taking money out.

Even if these savings account options aren't going to make you rich off of interest, it does set up some discipline so you have to start saving. Additionally, your money is protected and insured. Don't let your savings be stolen when that ceramic piggy bank suddenly goes missing; protect your investment to yourself and open one of the savings accounts I mentioned.

Set Up Automated Savings

In the world we currently live in, we love automation. There are automated vacuums, cupcake ATMs, and even robots that help with surgery! So it shouldn't be too far off to suggest that you should have your savings taken out automatically. If you get a steady paycheck, you don't even see the portion that goes to your taxes. Because you never see it, you never spend that money.

What if creating automated savings was as easy as paying your taxes every paycheck you get? This is actually a very easy process and it can help you save hundreds or thousands of dollars a year. If you currently have direct deposit set up through your employer, you can request that a percentage of your check each month gets sent to another account. This makes it incredibly easy to save because it takes the spending temptation away.

If you have to move the money over to your savings each month, it is easy to find a way to spend the money instead of move it. However, if it is already taken out of your paycheck and deposited into your savings account, it's like you never had the money to begin with. Sure, it may seem like you are taking a bit of a pay cut, but what's better than building your savings?

If you want to get really fancy, you can even set up different savings accounts for different purposes. You can have your emergency fund, your fun fund, retirement fund, future children fund, etc. Each month you can divvy up your savings to each of these accounts and build them simultaneously.

Use Your Tax Refunds to Boost Your Savings

How excited do you get when tax refund season rolls around? With names such as Tax-mas, people see their tax refund as an opportunity for an all-out spending spree. It is a big chunk of money that you didn't plan on receiving. It's exciting!

But you know what could be even more exciting? If you rolled that money into a savings account or an investment fund. While I'm not an investment guru, putting your tax refund into a savings account as an "investment" is a much better choice than blowing it at the mall. You can give yourself an even bigger return by allowing it to continue to grow.

Whether you decide to put that refund into a retirement account, a savings account, or use it to learn the tricks and trades of the stock market, your future is going to thank you. It is also a great way to put a down payment on your debt. If you currently are struggling to get out of debt, put half of your refund into savings and half of it toward your debt.

Monitor Your Spending

Boys and girls, if you don't manage your money and monitor your spending, you are buying a one-way ticket to Debtsville. Seriously, you will never be able to get out of debt if you do not monitor your spending habits. Sure, a dollar coffee here and a dollar soda there doesn't seem like a ton of money, but do this once or twice a day and you can spend close to $1,000 dollars over the year. While the thousand bucks a year for coffee and snacks doesn't sound as much as $2,000 for the newest Macbook or iPhone, it still matters. Saving both of these amounts would save you $3,000 a year. That's not a bad amount for savings.

In order to save your money, you have to monitor your spending. The good news is that in this day and age, there are about a million different ways for you to monitor your spending.

There are companies like Mint that have both a website (mint.com) and an app. Personal Capital is also a great choice. There are even apps like Acorn that help you save by making all of your purchases even and saving your extra change. For example, if you bought a donut that was $1.35, acorn would charge your account $2.00 and then put the $0.65 into savings. While it may not seem like much, this can add up to a good chunk of money over the year without you lifting a finger.

The most important way to monitor your spending is to create a budget. Budgets are important for every person and business out there. Companies wouldn't survive without budgets in place! In the next chapter, I'll break down exactly why you need a budget and how you can budget your finances to quickly get out of the debt cycle.

Chapter 7: How to Create a Budget

Creating a budget is important to get yourself out of debt, or to keep yourself from getting into debt again, but so many people struggle with creating a budget and sticking to it. With our never-ending pace, it can be hard to actually budget out our money. Once you budget, you will be glad that you did.

The budgeting methods I'll talk about are zero-based budgeting methods and alternative budgeting methods.

What does "zero budgeting method" mean? It means that you are giving every dollar a job. Zero-based budgeting literally comes with the tagline "give every dollar a job." To explain it further, it means that you budget every dollar of your income to exactly match your expenses.

Now, wait up a second, this doesn't mean that you get to spend every dollar you make! This budgeting takes your income and divides it among your expenses, including the money you are putting into your savings account. This method is perfect for those who want to completely control their money. Using this method, you can micromanage your money in a good way so that you know exactly where your money is going.

There are two different budgeting methods I'm going to talk about. If you are on a fixed income, I will present you the Mint budget concept. If you are on an income that varies per month, you can follow my own personal method to help you budget your income best.

Zero-based budgeting methods

Fixed Income

If you work the same amount of hours every week or you are paid on salary, you have a fixed income. When your income doesn't vary every check, you should have a pretty good handle on where each dollar goes. But it might be time to change how you are budgeting if you don't have good savings. For those with fixed incomes, I recommend Mint's budgeting concept.

Mint rolls out the 50/30/20 budget. It is a rule that you will live by! Basically, 50% of your income stands for your essential expenses, 30% could be used for personal expenses, and 20% should be put directly into your savings. These three things add up to 100% of your income without a dollar to spare. This is a great place to start your budgeting journey.

At first glance, you may think that 50% is a little high for your essentials, but most people actually struggle with keeping their essentials to 50% of their income. Essentials include everything from your housing bills and student loans to debts, and even the butter on your morning toast! If you can stick to 50% for your essentials, you are doing a great job.

Obviously, if these numbers don't work for you, they can be adjusted. Think of the 50/30/20 budget as a framework to your own budgeting. Maybe you only need 40% for essentials and you can add another 10% to savings. Or maybe you really need 60% for essentials and only 20% for personal expenses. No matter which way you divide your income, it is starting to save that is really important here.

Because this budget is dividing the income you already have, it is easily adaptable for many people. It also takes the guesswork out of budgeting. Instead of saving X amount of dollars a month, you are saving a percentage of your income. As your income grows, so does your savings! This is helpful because you don't have to keep track of the dollar amount you are putting into your savings each month.

When you develop a good budgeting system, you set yourself up for life. I'm a big believer in the idea that if you give a man a fish, then he eats for a day, but if you teach a man to fish, he eats for life. I'm trying to teach you to fish for yourself! These budgeting habits will help you to get out of debt and then stay out of it.

Now it's time to divide your own income. You didn't think I was going to let you get off that easy, did you? Grab a sheet of paper and a pen. Write down the amount of money you receive each paycheck. Whether this is weekly, bi-monthly, or every month depends on your job.

Let's say you make $1,000 a paycheck and you get paid every two weeks. So for the two weeks, you have $500 for essentials, $300 for personal expenses, and you're going to be putting $200 into your savings account.

Remember that piece of paper you had with all of your monthly expenses written down? Go and grab it. Look at these numbers and look at what you get paid each paycheck. Do the numbers match up? Will you be able to fit your expenses into these percentages?

If your essentials are taking up 60% of your income and you are spending the other 40% on personal expenses, it's time to cut out a few things. Maybe that means you go a few weeks longer before going to the hair salon, or cutting out your twice-weekly bar night. The personal expense category is where you can cut out a lot of unnecessary items.

The goal here is to get as much as you can into your savings. By saving more, you set yourself up for less debt down the road.

Variable Income

Because I'm living the entrepreneurial life, I never know what I'm going to be making. This can be really stressful if you don't have a good grip on your spending habits. Not every month will be my best month. I have to be prepared — mentally and financially — to survive the shoestring months. I'm lucky in one aspect, though: I get paid with a sixty-day delay. This means that I know sixty days in advance what I am going to make two months later. This allows me to forecast and plan my budget far ahead of time without any hiccups.

Even if you are unsure what you are going to be paid, you can still categorize your expenses in other ways. My personal budgeting method can help with this.

The budgeting method I present consists of six different categories. These categories are food, entertainment, clothes and cosmetics (gentlemen, feel free to change this), business, travel, and other. Each of these categories has a strict cap, and I take it very seriously. I never spend beyond my cap! I chose these categories because they cover my lifestyle's expenses the best. If you hardly ever travel, or you don't fight a vicious fight with post-adolescent pimples, you might not need the same categories. Travel, however, doesn't necessarily mean taking a flight to Tuvalu. It can be your monthly gas consumption, bus tickets, bike tire change — you name it. Choose categories that best suit your needs.

Individuals with variable incomes have a hard time spending. As the game goes, when you make more money, you spend more. In fact, many people who experience positive change in their income by making more through a promotion or inheritance, or even winning the lottery, end up increasing their demands. When you start earning a little more, you end up springing for the more expensive salami or buying a piece of clothing that's not on sale, and pretty soon, you're back to where you started.

News flash: This is a horrible way to manage your money. People who do this are in the spending mindset instead of the savings mindset. In order to keep yourself out of the confines of debt, you have to keep yourself in a savings mindset.

Let me share a funny story with you. One of my clients asked me for financial advice during one of our sessions. This client is a genuinely kind-hearted, good person, however, he likes to flash his stuff. He is struggling with deep-rooted insecurities and thinks his gadgets will make him more desirable and interesting. One day we were talking about his spending habits and he told me that he never makes it through the month on his salary. He accumulates debt each month. I told him the difference between the saving mindset and the spending mindset and he was bewildered.

Some years ago, he went to some financial course taught by a self-proclaimed "guru" where he was told that if he wanted to become rich, he had to start acting like rich people do. He should believe, imagine, or visualize (whatever) that he was rich already. What did our friend do? He started adopting this flashy, spendthrift lifestyle, pretending he was rich. When I told him that rich people actually have a saving mindset and poor people have the spending mindset, he was shocked.

Most of us mistakenly think that the saving mindset is what poor people have. They are all about saving money, stressing their soul out because of the lack of money. But how do they start each day of their life? "What do I need to spend on today?" or, "what can I buy today?" or, "What can I afford today?" These questions reflect different levels of a scarcity-spending mindset.

People who wake up thinking how much they can save or make are those who sooner or later won't have financial headaches. Not everybody becomes a billionaire, but that's not even the goal of personal financing. The goal of personal financing is keeping more money in your pocket than your monthly expenses. Personal finances help you develop a healthy financial mindset and help you to never have money issues again.

You want billions? You should read another book for that. Oh, and sacrifice your entire life for the sake of it, because regardless of what you hear, big money comes with a high price. Anyone who tells you that you don't have to work hard for good money is either scamming you or does something fishy for a living. Honest, real, legal money comes with a lot of work.

Back to our reality: Even if you have a good month, you need to keep the savings mindset. Don't worry, the savings mindset makes rich people rich, and poor people rich too. The simplest method to save money and gain back financial freedom is to budget. Some of my months are really great and others are pretty bad. So how do I manage to save?

It comes pretty easy. I decide how much of my income I want to save and I plan accordingly. I pay myself first. Through this, I often save around 40-50% of my income, but some of my categories have very low caps in order to let me do this.

Yes, you read correctly. I have a category called "other." If you are wondering what the "other" category is, it is the unpredictable category that is supposed to cover unexpected expenses. This is the only category without a cap. I could also call it "emergency expenses." For example, last month I was enjoying my day out on the ocean and when I leaned a little too far off the boat, my phone slipped, and the tragedy of this situation is I had to buy a new phone. Believe me, I gave myself a lot of flak for that stupid mistake. Thankfully, though, I could afford to buy a new phone with the money I had saved previously. That month my "other" category expense was painfully high. Regularly, however, that category stays below $100.

I tried to stay positive about the incident, though. Shit happens. And while a waterlogged phone is certainly annoying, at least I wasn't draining my savings for something worse, like an illness or an accident. I also had some savings that made the purchase possible. You can always find an upside in the downsides that you can be thankful for.

So, how do I keep track of what I spend? I use this very advanced software called Excel. Obviously, I'm joking; Excel is a great tool to use for your budgeting and pretty much everyone already has it on their computer. Every expense and all the money I have coming in go into my Excel chart. I set up the automatic division for the number of cells I have, and when I spend something, the

Excel sheet automatically calculates my remaining "fortune."

I use Excel because it is cheap to use, quick to learn, and a transparent budgeting method. Once you set it up correctly, you can use it until the day you die. Lucky you, right? Seriously, though, it's a great budgeting tool. Here's a screenshot of my Excel spreadsheet:

As you can see in the top corner, I have what's called a Running Balance. There's a box where I add up all of my earnings and another box that has all of my spending. I use the "Description" for my categories. Each category is color-coded and each color gets separately calculated. The BALANCE chart shows the current amount of money that I have and the Monthly Recurring Expenses is where you have fixed expenses like debt (thankfully, I don't have any more!).

2017			
Jan-01	(food)		Monthly Food Budget:
Jan-02	(travel)		Monthly Entertainment:
Jan-02	(other)		Monthly Business Cost:
Jan-02	(food)		Monthly Travel Cost:
Jan-03	(business)		Monthly Other Costs:
Jan-03	(entertainment)		Monthly Clothes Cost:

The second chart I'm showing you above illustrates what my first few expenses were for the month of January 2017. You can see the different color-coded categories in play here and how at the beginning of the month, I assign a cap estimate to each category. This is what you will need to do for each and every month. Some months you may need to buy a new item of clothing, and the next month you may not need to buy any at all! This is completely up to your discretion, and I believe that the six categories I use really encompass everything you need.

At the end of each month, I compare my estimates with the actual amount spent. In most cases, they will match within a few dollars. Give yourself a little wiggle room, but try to never spend beyond your cap. If you don't take the category caps seriously, you might as well not be budgeting at all.

Also, if you own a black and white Kindle, let me help you out with category colors. I use green for

Food, Business is red, Entertainment is orange, Travel is purple, Clothes is gray, and Other is blue. I chose colors at random and you can too. Just make sure to stick with the same colors every month so you don't wind up confusing yourself!

If you use this budgeting method, I know you will see an improvement in your savings and spending habits. However, this method isn't the only way you can budget your income. There are plenty of options and plans to follow.

Alternative Budgeting Methods

Values-Based Budget

For example, you can always budget with the values-based budget. What this budgeting method does is takes what is important to you and you budget based off of what you like. Let's say you love to travel, if that is one of your values, so you want to create a traveling fund.

If you consider yourself a foodie, maybe you have a large fund for eating out and trying new restaurants. However, if you are a techie, you would save your money for the newest gadget that just hit the shelves. This budgeting system is all about spending money on what is important to you and saving money on the things that aren't as important to you.

If you find yourself an already money-savvy person, this budget may be perfect for you.

Tracking every dollar may seem a little too constrictive for your personality, and there's nothing wrong with that! But this budget is really up to your discretion. If you don't spend your money well, this budgeting tool will probably be hard for you to follow. You don't have set limits or percentages to work with, so be aware of that as you try it out. I recommend this budgeting method only if you are debt-free, have some savings, and your monthly money flow allows you to be a financially aware person (although if you are debt-free and have savings, that's a good sign). This type of budgeting is fun and value-oriented.

Cash-Only Budget

I know what you're thinking: Why would you carry around cash? In a world where cash seems to be an almost obsolete form of currency, it may be strange to think that you would carry cash instead of just swiping your card. But that's actually what will save you money. If every time you bought something you had to hand over cash, you would not spend nearly as much as you spend when you swipe a card. Why? Because you actually see the money leaving.

When we swipe our cards at the store, it's just that. A swipe. We don't see the actual money being handed over and it becomes easy to buy something when all you have to do to purchase it is swipe your card. With this budget, you go to the bank and pull out all the cash you need for your expenses. Once the cash is gone, it's gone, so you better budget well.

Once you pull out cash for your expenses, you divvy the money up into categories like groceries, gas, and entertainment. Whatever you do, you pay for it in cash. If you are a chronic spender, this can help you budget because once that cash is out, it's out. This is a good method for people who may not spend as much money or don't have a lot of money to spend, like college students and young professionals.

Chapter 8: Advice for Women

All right, women, this chapter is all for you! Gentlemen can also find some good nuggets here, but I dedicated this chapter to ladies for a good reason.

Did you know that women ask for less financial advice than men do? This completely surprises me because men can be a little stubborn when it comes to asking for help. Finances should not be something that we are afraid to learn about and own!

A recent survey by Country Financial found that 23.6% of women never ask for financial advice compared to just 15.2% of men. And when women do ask for advice, it is mostly for retirement planning. But still, only 37% of women asked about retirement savings whereas 45% of men asked for retirement advice.

It's no unknown fact that women live longer than men. In fact, we live on average five years longer than men! So shouldn't we be asking a little bit more about retirement financial planning since we'll be living longer? Yeah, I think so! But still, women are afraid to ask.

Why is this? It might have something to do with the fact that women on average only make approximately 83 cents for every dollar that a man makes. The gender pay gap is a well-known issue, and yet it hasn't changed much over the years. It just goes to show that women don't speak up about money.[vi]

The Financial Ostrich

Have you ever heard someone say that when an ostrich is afraid, they stick their head in the sand? Picture an ostrich with its head buried in the sand. Now, I hate to be the one to tell you that this precious saying is actually a myth, but the image still rings true. Women often stick their head in the sand when it comes to finances. Is it because we don't know as much? Or have smaller brains, as Will Farrell stated in a very bad rom-com? Absolutely not. It's because we get afraid.

The time has come to stop being afraid of asking and seeking out financial advice. What excuses have you made for avoiding asking for financial advice? Is it that you've convinced yourself that you are bad with numbers? Do you rely on your partner to do the math? Maybe you trust your financial advisor and believe everything they say, or maybe finances are just dull and unsexy to you.

Whatever your reason, financial ignorance is not bliss. If you bury your head in the sand, a sunny day is going to come and you're going to get burned. Staying financially unaware is dangerous! You probably trust your spouse. If you don't, that's a whole different book to read. But even if you don't think you need to know about dirty money because your spouse is golden, you still need to.

In today's world, a basic financial education is essential. Even if you aren't currently pulling in an income of your own, understanding how money comes and goes, how your taxes work, and how your savings work is important to your future.

If you haven't seen the movie "The Other Woman," I highly recommend it. It's a hilarious comedy which follows the women of a man who is a serial cheater. The wife of this man finds out that her husband is using her signature to transfer illegal money offshore. When she thinks she is signing utility bills or basic paperwork, she has no idea she is actually committing a crime.

Sure, this situation doesn't happen every day, but still, we women need to be prepared. It's quite a funny movie and just shows that a naïve woman won't be living the greatest life.

Finances Before Marriage

Did you know up to 90% of marriages that fail can be contributed to money issues? How someone views money is extremely important. If you are looking into marrying someone, you have to know what they believe and think about finances. If you aren't on the same page, issues will only become more and more divisive as the marriage goes on.

People will talk about everything else before a marriage like sex, drugs, and rock and roll, but they refuse to talk about their finances. Our society has a hard time talking about finances. Many of us view money as a symbol of power, control, security, or love. The last thing you want to happen is to have a fairytale wedding and then realize money is about to break you apart.

Talk about your finances with your partner before you get married. Know what to expect from each other. If you start to see warning signs or red flags, it is probably a good idea to step out of engagement bubble and look at if this relationship can work out with different money views. It is much easier to call something off before a marriage than after. Follow these ten tips below so you aren't caught off-guard with finances in your marriage.

1. One rule is to not take on another person's debt. Debt is stressful. Taking on another person's debt is even more stressful! Wait until you and your partner are debt-free before you tie the knot. If the debt is too substantial or you don't want to wait to be married, consider signing a prenuptial agreement. While we often think of them for the rich, it can actually be a good idea for everyone.

2. If you are already married, take an active role in your family's finances. Talk to your spouse about

money and familiarize yourself with your personal finances. It is much easier to get through a storm you are aware of instead of going into one unprepared. If there isn't a money issue currently on hand, you can have a calm and relaxed discussion about it. This will help you understand what is going on if another issue arises down the road.

If you aren't used to broaching the subject of finances, it can help to voice your feelings about a financial issue in the relationship. Even something as simple as, "I worry I might be spending too much on our grocery bill" can lead to a deeper conversation. If you find an issue you cannot agree on, try to compromise. If you respect each other and your relationship, it can be easy to negotiate.

Some women who have been independent may fear being taken care of in a relationship. You might even be worried about losing the money you have worked hard for, or maybe your partner has some spending habits you are uncomfortable with. If you are honest with yourself and your partner about what you are feeling, you are paving the road to a stronger and healthier relationship.

3. Keep yourselves to a budget and find a number that fits both of your expectations. Compromise will need to happen, especially if one person loves to spend money and the other doesn't. If you want to, you can always keep separate credit cards and bank accounts and then have a joint account where you put all your expense money in. This can help to restrain each person from spending more money than there is in the expense account.

An important rule when you marry is to not give in to social pressure. You might have some couple friends who are always buying high-end items and pressuring you to keep up with them. Don't give in! This will ruin your budget and can cause feelings of resentment with your spouse. If you use the money to make yourself feel good at the literal and proverbial expense of the other, your marriage will suffer. You don't need that Louis Vuitton bag just because Cindy has it. Learn to spend quality time with your spouse instead of shopping or impulse buying.

4. Strive to educate yourself financially. Whether you use Google as your professor or read some financial books, do what you can to make sure that you know how finances work.

Also, strive to create financial goals with your spouse. When you work together toward better finances, no one is surprised or hurt when financial issues arise. It is important for women to take an active role in their family's financial planning. Even if it's something as simple as meeting every week for ten minutes to go over your budget and bank statements, do it!

5. Research is your friend, and it will help you out! Research every product before you buy it, especially if it is expensive. If you purchase everything in the store, you could be costing yourself money. Online stores are now so competitive that you can often find a cheaper deal or price match to get the best price. The least you can do is try to find a coupon before you buy.

6. If you have an inheritance or you decide to invest in something, keep it in your name. While it may sound distrustful to a spouse, money is a business matter, not a relationship matter. It is

easy to keep your own investments. You can always have investments with your spouse as well, but you should also have your own investments in your name.

7. It is never too soon to think about what you need to do for retirement. If you are in your twenties or thirties, this probably sounds crazy! But, life gets busy. Life starts to pass you by, and before you know it, you're going to need that retirement fund. Start thinking about it now and take advantage of compound interest.

Even a small amount invested now can grow to an impressive retirement fund due to compound interest. Don't put your faith in social security. Take your future into your own hands and invest in your retirement.

8. Do you volunteer your time? Maybe you teach your friend's child after work or help tutor the neighbor. If you do this in addition to working your sixty hours a week job, yes, you're a nice person. But nice girls finish last. They don't get rich — they get taken advantage of. Do you really want to be taken advantage of? No.

You have to start charging for your services. If you have a skill set, so don't sell yourself short and do it for free. Think of it as a business. If you charge people for this service, they are going to appreciate the work you do much more. Plus everyone charges for their work. Even if you only charge a little, your skills are your livelihood! Own them and respect yourself. Your time and knowledge are worth the buck.

9. Have you ever been to a garage sale and wanted an item, but it was a little too pricey? I bet you have. And I bet you bargained for that item and got it for a great price. As you walked away with your new mint-condition item, you felt accomplished and you knew you had scored.

Negotiation skills are invaluable in many ways. If you know how to negotiate, you can save yourself time and money. You'll get better deals and you'll be more respected. When you are ready to negotiate, people know they can't BS around you. And yet so many of us have a hard time negotiating.

Girl, it's time to get down to business! Learning to negotiate will help you in more ways than you can dream. Don't fret if the thought of negotiating scares you — you can learn! Check out the books *Crucial Conversations, Getting More,* and *Never Split the Difference.* These books can teach you everything you need to know about negotiating and how to become more comfortable with it.

10. Family and friends pressuring us are the worst. How many dance recitals or holiday parties have you been dragged to against your will because someone in your family pressured you? Too many to count, on my end. But what's worse than a dreadful holiday party is getting yourself into an awkward situation by borrowing money from family or friends or loaning it out to them.

I'm a big believer that when you take someone's money, you are opening yourself to take their input. Borrowing or loaning out to family and friends can blur boundaries. It makes parties awkward if you haven't paid them back or they haven't paid you back. Plus it's super-awkward to ask for that money back or ask them to hurry up on their loan payments if they miss a month. You might need that money, and without collateral backing the loan, you won't have anything you can do. Save yourself the relationship ruin and resist borrowing or loaning out money.

Chapter 9: 30 Quick Financial Tips

Don't worry, I'm not leaving you that fast! Before this financial advice comes to a close, I'll leave you with 30 tips that will continue to help you. If you follow what you've learned, you can step out of the debt epidemic and find yourself financially free.

1. Don't invest in multi-level marketing. Ever. Seriously, don't. Not only do you have to pay money to get started in this business, but finding people to buy your product is hard! You end up making too little a commission on the product to really make any money. It may seem tempting when you see the social media posts of the top-earners, but succeeding in multi-level marketing is really a one in a million chance. And I hate to be the one to break it to you, but you won't make your millions this way. You will just alienate your friends

and family — your initial target "customers."

2. Don't buy a new car if your car still works. Read your car's instruction manual. Sure, it may seem fairly obvious, but if you take care of your car, it will last a lot longer. Cars depreciate by one third of their value the minute you drive them off the lot. So while you can, take care of it and use it for yourself.

3. But don't fill your car up on premium gas. This is like snake oil to drivers. Your car will function and run perfectly on the regular gas that it needs. Unless it's an absolute necessity for the car you drive, skip the premium.

4. The chances of your electronics breaking down and needing those extended warranties are really slim. That's why those policies are so cheap! They're easy money-makers for these electronics sellers. You will be fine without them. Most electronics have a free one-year guarantee. The two to three year

warranties might seem like a good idea, as one would assume stuff gets broken after the first year more easily. Usually, however, these extended warranties have lots of terms and conditions. They will only fix your three-year-old robot vacuum cleaner if it fell off the stairs of its own volition at a thirty-five degree angle while crying for help. You need to prove your claim to a ridiculous degree. Plus if something breaks, you can easily get it fixed for the same price as what the extended warranty cost.

5. Motrin is still ibuprofen, no matter how popular the name. Ask for the generic versions of medications in pharmacies. They have the same exact active ingredients and are much cheaper.

6. One of the best things you can do to save yourself money is to bring your lunch to work! You can spend thousands of dollars a year eating out for lunch. Thousands! So do yourself a favor and bring your own lunch.

7. While I don't recommend buying many items, a fireproof safe is really important. It will keep your most important documents safe from harm, and you can keep some cash in there as well.

8. When something breaks, don't immediately throw it out. Before you go out and spend money on something new, see if what you already have might be fixable. Things like high-end electronics or pricey shoes may be cheaper to fix than to buy new. If you can save yourself money this way, do it.

9. Something important to more than just your finances is to read your contracts. Every contract you sign should be thoroughly read. I know, it's long and the wording is hard to understand, but save yourself time and trouble by reading through every segment and line that there is. The last thing you want to do is to be caught off guard and surprised when you breach a contract.

10. Learning basic mechanic and plumbing skills will help you immensely. If there's not a risk of electrocuting yourself or breaking something further, you can often fix the problem with a little help. Thanks to the Internet, you can find tutorials for anything! Clogged toilets, dripping sinks, and an oil change are all things that you can easily learn to do. Skills like these will save you money throughout your whole life.

11. If you love to read, you're my kind of person! However, buying a lot of books can add up over the years. Library cards are free. You can read lots of books that are available at your local library. If you love to collect the books you read, buy them used. Sure, this may mean you need to wait a few weeks after a new one is released to buy it, but you can save yourself up to 80% of the cost of it new!

12. When you are opening a bank account, have a checking and a savings account. A savings account doesn't give you immediate access to swipe your card at

the store and can save you from overspending.

13. When you are filing your taxes, an accountant is a must. Even throughout the year, an accountant can help you get your finances under control. The amount of money they save you will easily be worth the cost of a few hours with them.

14. If you can, try to use cash more often. As I explained in the budgeting chapter, you will spend more money if you use a card. When you have to hand over physical cash, you will spend less.

15. If you want to buy something, wait 30 days. If you can wait 30 days and still want the item, it might be on sale and cheaper. In any case, you at least know it's an item you really want. This will help cut down on impulse purchases. I don't mean a single donut or a pen; I mean the more expensive items — let's say things that cost $30 or more (based on your income, you can redefine what is expensive).

16. Meal planning is a great way to save money. If you meal plan, you know exactly what you will be making and you will spend less money at the grocery store. You only buy what you need so you won't be wasting food and costing yourself more money there.

17. Go through your closet every few months and get rid of the clothing you don't wear. You can take it to consignment shops, sell it, and have a little extra cash for buying the new clothes that you need. You can also sell your stuff on eBay. Did you hear of the book or Netflix series *Girl Boss*? The heroine built a million-dollar brand by selling used clothes on eBay.

18. When it's time to get yourself a different car, consider buying used. Buying a used car can save you thousands of dollars. Many cars that are only two or three years old are still in great condition and have fewer miles than you think.

19. When the holidays come around, consider making some homemade gifts. Knit a scarf,

create spice mixes or cookie mixes, or make your own gift baskets! These homemade gifts aren't just sentimental; they can also be one of the best gifts a person can receive. Who doesn't like homemade cookies?

20. If you are a city-dweller, consider dropping a car altogether and taking public transit! Public transportation can be pretty cheap and an easy way to get you where you need to be. Plus you get extra time to sit instead of driving through the horrific traffic. You can use this extra time to read, get things done, or plan your budget.

21. Now, stay with me on this one. Cutting your hair can be a thrifty way to give yourself a trim. If you don't have a hard-to-style haircut, or you have closely shaved hair, skip the hairdressers. You can easily save yourself hundreds of dollars every year just by giving yourself a trim. I have a friend who is a literal millionaire, but he hasn't gone to a hairdresser in the past 20 years or so. He has a little hair cutting machine and a scissor and he does his own

hair every other week. He could certainly afford any hairdresser, but he finds it a stupid expense. Moreover, he likes how he does his hair. He doesn't trust others. He knows what he wants and does it.

22. If you want to save yourself some time and money, skip watching so much TV. Not only will you cut back on the ads that you see, but you'll also gain more time to do productive things around the house or pick up a side job.

23. If you have the storage space, you can save a lot of money by getting your holiday shopping done the year before. It sounds crazy, but think of the sales that happen the day after Valentine's, Easter, and Christmas! Use this time to stock up on those holiday decorations, cards, and maybe even a gift or two.

24. Check the ads for grocery stores that come in the mail. Different stores run different weekly specials, and you may be shopping at a more expensive store and not realizing it. By comparing the ads, you can choose

the least expensive store and save money. This may be a different store each week.

25. Switch out those old-style lightbulbs. While energy efficient lightbulbs may cost a few more pennies up front, they are going to save you in the long run. Not only do they last longer, they also burn less electricity. They are worth the initial investment for the amount of money they will save you.

26. Don't be afraid to check out yard sales and thrift stores! Seriously, these places are filled with clothes donated from massive over-spenders. People clear out their closets, and often enough, they have only worn the article of clothing a few times. One man's trash can be your treasure! Not only will you keep looking great, you'll also pay way less than the clothes are worth.

27. If you have a green thumb, start a small vegetable garden. While this is ideal if you have a yard, some veggies like lettuce and herbs can easily be grown in a planter in

an apartment or dorm room too. You're only as limited as you make yourself!

28. Want a more eco-friendly home while saving money? Try making your own cleaners. DIY cleaners contain just a few ingredients, and many of them use cheap staples like white vinegar to make your cleaning routine hassle-free and cheap.

29. Slow down! When you are driving, stop going over the speed limit. Not only do you risk getting a ticket, but you also burn more gas.

30. Go vegetarian (for a few meals, at least). Meat is the most expensive item on your grocery bill. Just by practicing Meatless Monday every week, you could be saving a good chunk of money. Skip the meat for a few meals and start saving!

Try to apply some of the advice received in this book to your life. Knowledge is only worthwhile if you use it. I can give you every tool to get out of debt, but it won't happen if you don't do something about it. You deserve to get yourself out of debt and onto the path of becoming financially free. I have been in your shoes, struggling to live on a small income day after day, I know how tough it is. My advice comes from profound and bitter experience. Whatever I preached here — I've been there, done that. I wasn't born a millionaire who is dispensing wisdom for the less fortunate while munching caviar in her Rolls-Royce.

If you stick to the advice laid out here, you will find yourself getting out of debt. Share your knowledge with your friends and family who also may be struggling with debt. The more people who find their way out of the debt epidemic, the closer we get to a more profitable society.

I hope you'll find your way out!

Yours,

Zoe

More Books By Zoe

Find What You Were Born For – Book 1
Find What You Were Born For – Book 2
Find Who You Were Born To Be
Catching Courage
Fearless
Daily Routine Makeover
Daily Routine Makeover – Morning Edition
Daily Routine Makeover – Evening Edition
Less Mess Less Stress
Braver Than You Believe
The Unlimited Mind
Wired For Confidence
Minimalist Makeover
Build Social Confidence
Discipline Your Mind

ommunication and Confidence Coaching

By working with me you can expect to gain a better understanding of yourself, and the hope you need to change your life for the better. I will help you understand everybody around you better starting with yourself. My three main goals are to help you:

- Embrace discomfort to break down your negative beliefs,
- Find your strengths and focus on them,
- Bring out the side of you that is totally comfortable with yourself and your environment.

I have a unique approach to coaching. The entire lesson is composed of two parts:

Interpersonal Skills Development

Do your palms sweat and your heart pound when you enter in a room full of strangers? Do you feel awkward when somebody starts a conversation with you? Do you fear you'll run out of things to say and wish you could just talk casually with everybody?

Then this course was made for you!

In this section, I'll help you learn how to communicate with others, how to be presentable, and how to always make a great impression. Humans are social beings and since you live among them you can never underestimate the importance of social skills. If you have them you can be 100-percent present and aware in any situation. I have been studying and developing communication and real-life social interaction skills for more than 10 years. I've written 10 books – all of them Amazon best-sellers – on the topic. I can help you, please let me!

Here you will learn:

• How to start conversations and keep them going with anybody,
• How to "win friends and influence people,"
• Airy, pleasant ways to be more charming and likable,
• How to be the life of the party, and
• Tips on how to handle difficult conversations and people.

I'll teach you how to be the person everyone notices when you enter the room, the person who instantly sparks people's interest and can talk easily to anyone.

Intrapersonal Skills Development

Is the mirror your worst enemy? Or the scale? Or both? Do you feel uncomfortable with who you are? Do you sometimes feel your days are passing by without any purpose? Is sleeping your favorite activity? Do you wish you were somewhere else, maybe someone else?

If any of these statements apply to you then you have work to do. Living with self-contempt, regrets, and frustration is not sustainable. In this part of the coaching I will help you to accept and recover from any inner struggles you have. With honesty and commitment, I will guide you to let go of old wounds, and help you find your strengths and develop them in order to bring out the best in yourself.

I'll help you:

- to discover the root cause of your problems,
- recover from childhood traumas,
- communicate with yourself objectively and silence

the malicious voices in your head,

- build confidence and self-respect, and learn to be persistent and get what you want.

Endnotes

[i] LSL. "What is a financial blueprint?" LSL. 2016. http://www.lslcpas.com/wp-content/uploads/2016/11/WM_Financial_Blueprint-1.pdf

[ii] NAPFA. "Americans Need To Understand What Financial Planning Is And How It Can Help: NAPFA introduces new infographic on the important role of financial planning." NAPFA. 2012. https://legacy.napfa.org/UserFiles/File/ImportanceofFinancialPlanningRelease100312.pdf

[iii] New Jersey Council For Economic Education. "Developing Economic and Financial Skills in New Jersey Students." New Jersey Council For Economic Education. 2013. http://newjersey.councilforeconed.org/wp-content/uploads/sites/2/2013/11/NJCEE-Overview-2013.pdf

[iv] Johnson, Angela. "76% of Americans are living paycheck-to-paycheck." CNN. 2013. http://money.cnn.com/2013/06/24/pf/emergency-savings/index.html

[v] Langagger, Chad. „How is my credit score calculated?" Investopedia. 2017.
http://www.investopedia.com/ask/answers/05/creditscorecalculation.asp

[vi] MoneyTips. "Men More Likely Than Women To Ask For Financial Advice." Globe Gazette. 2017.
http://globegazette.com/business/investment/personal-finance/men-more-likely-than-women-to-ask-for-financial-advice/article_facd8932-b435-5074-9928-5619c6657603.html